JACKAL & WOLVES
BY
MIKE MATHER

FTW

Forever Two Wheels

My colors are Black, Red, and White.

Black is strength, war, and death.

Red is blood, strength, and power.

White is purity, innocence, and perfection.

Warriors train for war wit strength, agility, and honor. protect the innocent and are prepared to shed blood with purification by death to evil.

Disclaimer; Neither the author or publisher assumes any responsibility use or misuse of the information in this book. Information in this book is distributed "as is" without warranty. Nothing in this document constitutes legal opinion nor should any of its contents be treated as such. Further, neither does the author or publisher have any control over or assume any responsibility for websites or external references in this book.

©2024 Mike Mather, Mather Martial Arts
All Rights Reserved - Compiled in the United States of America first Release Date May 2024

Contacting Mike Mather

Email; guromwm@gmail.com
mail; PO BOX 66
Columbia City, OR 97018

Table of Contents

Dedication	6
Introduction	7
Acknowledgment	8
Forwards/opinions	12
Predators - Jackals and Wolves	28
When the predator attacks	33
Fighting ranges	39
The beginning stages of my Martial life	44
Personal experience	53
My time with the Hells Angels	79
Awareness and what I carry	86
Situational Tutorial	103
Training in different environments	134
Wolves	138
My Martial Arts BIO	151
Warriors Code	158

DEDICATION

To my dad, my hero, Kenneth Wayne Mather for being a man of men and passing on the road map of what it is to be a warrior. To the code

INTRODUCTION
JACKAL AND WOLVES

My name is

Sifu Mike Mather

I've been fighting since the day I was born. I come from Viking descent so I've always had this inner feeling to be a protector at all costs. No one ever gets hurt on my watch. This is my expression and opinion on how to handle yourself and/or prepare yourself for a street fight against one or multiple people. I love all systems of martial arts but I feel most are lacking in reality training.

Let me start by saying there is no perfect road map. My opinion is based on personal experience, continuous study, and understanding how the predators think, act, and prey. I do not think by any means that I am the toughest person out there. I feel I am a white belt 24/7 always willing to learn. I've changed my way of fighting 100 times over. Remember this one thing there is always someone tougher out there.

The most under estimated thing out there is a man's heart. What is the length of pain he is willing to endure before he reaches his quitting point. This also goes for you. How much pain can you take before you give in? The answer is when your six feet under you'll stop. I will always go home at night. The old saying is I'd rather be judged by 12 than carried by 6.

ACKNOWLEDGMENT
Paying Respect Where Respect is Due

Instructors in my life

Every warrior needs guidance in life to learn how to become a man of honor, integrity, respect, wisdom, skill and most important a man with heart. These men below have all played an important roll in this.

GM Dan Anderson is a very special friend of mine. I've known of him my whole life in training martial arts. He has always been an instructor I looked up to. He is one of the best martial artists in the NW. He analyzes and dissects everything martial so that he is the best at what he does. I have been greatly blessed and honored to have such a great warrior helping with the publishing of this book. It would not have had near the impact and professionalism without his help. Thank you dan we are forever connected.

Your brother Sifu Mike

My beautiful wife Ruth Mather. Without her who knows where I would be today. She came into my life in late 2004. Shortly after in May of 2005 I broke my back in five places. I was in bed for a year. I couldn't bend over. I could barely walk without excruciating pain. She helped me fight through all my fears and pains. I was able to start training again and continue my educations in martial arts. I will be forever be thankful to Ruth. My true Soul Mate. My Ride or Die. My Queen. She helped make this book all possible .

FORWARDS/OPINIONS

Mike Mather has been a brother of mine for some time. Recently I got a call from him asking if I would help him with the book you hold in your hands, Jackal & Wolves. I said yes and I am glad I did. I have come away far better educated.

These days, people tend to specialize in their approach to martial arts. This, by the way, is the pot calling the kettle black. I specialized in both competition karate and Filipino stick fighting. Anyone who knows me knows that I excelled in these ventures and am somewhat of an authority in them. As an authority in these facets of the arts, I also recognize where I am not an authority. This is where Mike comes in.

Mike is an authority in mean streets application. Let me put it this way – when Mike speaks about street application of the martial arts, I shut up, listen, and learn a lesson or two.

I learned many lessons editing this book. Blow past this forward and get into this book. I'll bet you'll be adding to your own toolbox.

This book is worth the read,

Prof. Dan Anderson
10th Dan - Karate
10th Dan - Presas Legacy Arnis

The first picture was taken at Mike Mathers early gym in Warrenton, OR around 2000. Marty Maye, Mike Rethati, Jerry Weldon, Gary LaRiviere and myself were all there. I remember some things about the day: It was one of our regular meetings to spar and spar and spar. We all enjoyed the hell outa each other. We would mix in some street moves with rough play also, while the guys sitting out would provoke the goings on with cat calls. There was some extra pride or crazy in the room that day, and not much quit. Mike really impressed me with his wicked jump spin hook kick. A technique executed with such immediacy, speed, and explosive power I could feel my neck hurt just watching him warm up. I remember thinking, he can hit Marty or Rethati, but he's not hitting me! I know I whispered something into Mike's ear like, better finish me with it, or I'm takin' ribs. All part of the game and we went away with hugs and laughter as always.

Second picture is Mike and I not long after reconnecting in 2017. Year's passed, yet we slipped right into our play; but as older gentleman we enjoyed coffee first! I may have went home with a black eye that day. The first time I really spoke with Mike's Father was during Ruth and Mike's wedding reception.

The music was loud and we were enjoying watching my son and Mike's daughter dance, while Marty provoked that situation. Mike's Dad walks right at me, I shake his hand and he says: Stick with Mike.

It was a curious comment from a man I barely know? Days later Mike explained to me, my Dad is my best friend and he told you that because he knows everything about you. He knows we are better together.
Mike's just one of these guys who's way is a joy to be around. I thank his Father's advice. He's a dear friend.

Tim Gustavson

PIC #1   PIC #2

I've known Mike Mather for over 30 years. I've taught him many things over the years. As a martial artist he is no nonsense and to the point. Trains very hard

Mike Mather has integrity, tenacity, and humility. He will stand by you as a true friend and human being

Sifu Eric Lee

Eric Lee and myself

I met Sifu Mike 30 years ago I was Teaching Kali an ARNIS at GM Al Dacascos gym. Al and I have been Great Friends for a long time. He has been Helping me promote Filipino martial Arts for a long time.

Mike loved What I was teaching. The weapons Double Sticks, single stick, double dagger, single dagger, and Bali song Mike trained with me to earn high Black belts In ARNIS & Kali.

We have become Brothers in the arts. Mike is one of my heavy hitters very powerful. My credentials are seventh-degree black belt under Roberto Presas Modern ARNIS . I'm a 6th Degree in ARJUKEN Karate and ARNIS under GM ERNESTO Presas. I'm a Full Instructor under Guro Dan Inosanto in Kali / JKD.

Mike has proven to be a Great Fighter and Teacher. I wish I had 100 students like him. My Great friend, Student, and Brother in the arts. God bless him an his.

Guro John Bruce Daniels

I have known Sifu Mike Mather for about 13 years now. I have had the pleasure to hang out with him many times. I consider him my Brother and Family. I Know Sifu Mike through our shared love of Martial Arts and Motorcycles. Sifu Mike is a solid and respectful individual. I have put quite a few miles on my motorcycle with him by my side. He is like me when it comes to riding, we go as fast as possible in every situation. Lol. His riding style is like mine, crazy to say the least. By this I mean we split cars going over 100 and often use the emergency lane as an express lane. However his skill level always keeps him safe.

He has studied Martial Arts for many years and often teaches seminars. I'm impressed by his vast knowledge of Martial Arts as well as weapons training. He is a very respectful man, however he does not allow anyone to disrespect him, his family or his Brothers around him. I have had the pleasure to see him in action on more than one occasion when dealing with other idiots. He usually handles the situation quickly and discretely. Sifu Mike is definitely someone I would want to have my back in any altercation.

The thing that impresses me the most though is his love for kids and helping out the community. He often supports and shows off his children and their accomplishments. He also volunteers and helps out the community.

He has quite the following now as "The Grinch". Kids love to see him in his costume and on his motorcycle. Sifu Mike is as real as they come which is so rare in this day and age. I feel truly honored to call Sifu Mike my Brother.

Bobby Wilson

AKA "Joker Bobby" Gypsy Joker Motorcycle Club

GJ Bobby and me

I met Mike Mather around 1999 and he has since become a close brother to me in the Martial Arts as well as a good friend.

I have had 40 plus years teaching Martial Arts as well as competing in all the major contact sports in America and abroad, and I can definitively say that Mike Mather's book is very informative and a great read. If you study Martial arts or you are looking into learning more on how to protect yourself, and the mindset that is required to do so, I highly recommend you dive into this book. It is no nonsense approach to defending yourself!

Sincerely,

Kathy Long

5 X World Kickboxing Champion and Master in Kung Fu San Soo.

Kathy Long

Sifu Restita DeJesus (RUSTY), Sifu Mike Mather, and Kathy Long (KAT).

Mike Mather, The Early Days.

Every summer, the Karate school I trained at used to teach a Summer Karate Camp for the Parks Department.

It was very popular with kids of all ages and it was a great introduction to the art. One summer when I was about 14 or 15 years old, I was put in charge of working with 10-12 year olds. Children of that age are all full of energy but there was one kid that had unlimited energy. It was impossible to tire him out, and he had crazy athletic ability.

His name was Mike Mather and he was a handful but not in a disrespectful or disruptive way.

Mike was just very eager to learn Karate and willing try anything. I would try to work everyone to the point of exhaustion, but that was not possible with Mike. The summer camp was only a week or two long so we didn't have much time to work on anything but basic moves but by the end camp, Mike was doing multiple kicking combos, spinning hook kicks, flying side kicks and what ever I could throw at him. Since camp was only a few days, we didn't do much sparring but Mike was just different and would stay after practice so we could spar without pads of course. The kid just wouldn't stop and only fought back harder when he got kicked or punched. After camp was over, Mike would ride his bike on the back roads from Warren, to my mom's house in St. Helens to join me in bag work and sparring.

After getting blasted from one side of the garage to the other, Mike would get on his bike and ride home. He would do this three to four times a week for a couple years. Once Mike was old enough to drive and toughened up by years of wrestling, he would come over and we would train for hours. Some of those garage battles were pretty fierce and Mike would keep coming back for more. Later we became teammates and fought all over together in tournaments. Sometimes we would end up fighting each other for first or the grands

Marty Maye and myself

I've been blessed with many great mentors in my 34 years in various martial arts, but Sifu Mike Mather is one of a kind. They broke the mold when they made him.

He is an absolute expert in weapons and the striking arts and has continued his bjj training with a beginners mindset at my school. I consider Sifu Mike my instructor and mentor although he says he wants to be my top student.

I know you will learn many great self defense skills and philosophies in this book as my brother Sifu has taken me through his epic life stories and opened my eyes and reenergized me in the meaning of what he calls "martial life", which we tend to miss in bjj. It's my suggestion that every BJJ practitioner and everyone learn weapons and street striking to be prepared in all situations after my training with Sifu Mike.

Don Stoner
2nd degree
Brazilian Jiu Jitsu Black Belt

Sifu Mike lives by the same code my father taught me. My father was an ex-marine that was trained in Parris Island he fought during World War II as a Gunner in Douglas dive bomber he was a boxer on the Marine Corps boxing team he taught me as a young man how to use my hands and some self-defense that he learned in the Marine Corps when I started doing Shotokan karate he told me "you want to be a tough guy well go down to a bar buy a beer stare at somebody and tell them to go f*** themselves and you'll be in all the fights that you want". That's the best training you'll ever get so me being not the most brightest guy I went down and tried it out. The next thing I know I was rolling around on the floor with the guy after he punched me in my face. I learned after that, That martial arts training it's good but learning how to be a real fighter is more important. So, the moral of the story is, get the first one in and you'll be the first one out. Remember the code. Love and God bless you

Brothers for life

Master Jeff Langton

Mike Mather, a martial arts luminary hailing from the Northwest, with an illustrious career in full-contact combat since 1986. His enduring commitment to martial arts serves as a beacon for those seeking to make a lasting impact in the community. Behind the rugged exterior of his Harley Davidson chopper and Grinch during festive seasons lies a loving family man deeply rooted in a legacy of discipline passed down from his father.

Mike's latest book unveils the secrets to becoming a holistic martial artist, covering everything from ground-and-pound techniques to adept weapon usage and self-defense strategies. Notably, his revolutionary concept of the Wolf mentality provides invaluable insights into handling multiple attacks, a true paradigm shift. "Mike Mather's inspirational training regimen, unwavering habits, and dedication serve as a beacon for all. Behind every successful man stands an equally formidable force, and in Mike's case, his biggest supporter is his wife, Ruth. Together, they exemplify a partnership that fuels not only personal success but also the collective spirit of dedication and support.

A devoted student across diverse martial arts forms and a cherished disciple of Sifu Al Dacascos, Mike's character and training style are synonymous with loyalty and authenticity. Embracing an old-school approach,

Mike Mather's training transcends the superficial, preparing individuals for the challenges of real-life situations. To follow in his footsteps is to embark on a journey towards martial arts excellence, where unwavering character and genuine skill converge." Mike remains a close friend and disciple of Sifu Al Dacascos

G.M. Al Dacascos and me holding 6th degree

PREDATORS

JACKAL and WOLVES

Predators

First off, there are two types of predators: a jackal and a wolf.

The jackal preys upon the weak.

A wolf will take on someone of equal or greater strength.

Now imagine a pack of jackals or a pack of wolves. Understanding the demeanor of both packs will help put that in perspective on how you train. I think a person needs to be proficient in all 5 ranges grappling, trapping, boxing, kicking, and projectile with or without weapons.

I've been competing. Fighting, and training my body pretty much since I came out the womb. I wouldn't change a thing especially in the order in which I learned the systems that help mold me into the Viking warrior I am today. Physical training is every bit as important as the skills themselves.

Some skills that I feel are valuable attributes to know require the strength of being able to pick a person up your own weight. Pull-ups and pushups have both been equally valuable exercises to me. Being strong at pushups develops a very powerful punch. Being strong at pull-ups develops a very strong grip and strength to pull someone towards you.

So, how do you understand the jackal or wolf? There is really no true way unless you run and play with the alpha predators. So, a Jackal preys upon the weak regardless man, women, or child. A pack of Jackals are still the same just in larger form with multiple attackers. But the difference is they are only strong in numbers and usually retreat when met with resistance. A lot of times what makes a group Jackals strong is the presence of a wolf that lost his way. Yes, that is correct a wolf will run with the jackals. He is most definitely the Alpha of the group. I also find it to be true that most jackals have had a rough upbringing as far as no role models, a good teacher to help them understand the trials and tribulations of life.

A wolf will meet any threat equal or greater size. There is no book written or instructional blue print that helps you understand a person that says "I CAN." What I mean by this, this is a person who stands up for what he believes and will protect his brother at all cost even if it means his life. I am my brother's keeper The place you can find wolves are places where a good martial code is taught. A person can be a wolf when raised by a family with all the virtues that a wolf possesses. Usually, most wolves come out of martial arts studios or the military. My whole life growing up I've been attracted to wolves. A wolf is a man that has honor, integrity, heart, and good morals.

I feel what makes a jackal or a wolf stems from childhood. It amazes me that a person can grow up to be a man or women without ever being punch in the face. Our society has coddled our kids over the last 30 years so they don't know how to deal with conflict. A kid needs to deal with conflict at a young age so he knows what it is to be respectful. Also, he needs to understand how people should be treated. This is how integrity, honor, and respect are created as a kid because kids today don't deal with conflict and are told to just tell or call the cops. It allows them to be disrespectful and not be held accountable for their actions. This is exactly how a jackal is created because as a kid, he picks on someone and even if the person sticks up for himself, they both get in the same amount of trouble. This can also have a reverse effect on the kid that was trying to be a good kid. He tries to do the right thing but still gets punished.

Kids solving problems the old school way

So, why would a kid want to do what's right when they get punished. The only thing that saves jackals today is having a good home structure and code to pass on and teach your kid. This same thing can create the bad wolf. Again, no accountability and sick of constantly failing. So, he trains to be the bigger bully whose had enough. Everyone has a snapping point in life. If you live by a code, it helps control, isolate and persevere through the trials and tribulations of life.

Most every street fight I've been in has been against more than one person. Since most of my life has been around guys that have their brother's back. I train to defend myself against that. Usually if a group of guys approaches you, they are most likely jackals so There is always one guy who is the talker, the instigator. He is always standing next to who he thinks or is the biggest or toughest guy in the group. That guy is usually a wolf that lost his code, his ethical road map and has chosen the wrong crowd to be around. **Sometimes a wolf will choose to hang around the jackals because it makes him feel superior.**

When the Predator attacks

HOW I REACT

When an altercation presents itself I will first put my back to a place no one can really get behind me very easily. Next thing I do is to take out the guy who is the quiet and intimidating guy standing next to the big mouth first. This is done with no hesitation and extreme prejudice. I want explode through him like a bazooka. I don't talk. I just react. Because he is usually the security blanket for the whole crew. When they see their toughest brother drop its an instant deflation in confidence. I might have to fight a couple more but usually they will run.

When the conflict has started, I am constantly changing elevation and direction using triangular footwork while striking in

ATTACKING THE THROAT AS AN ENTRY

The changing of elevation is done like a wrestling take-down or duck under. If any time I turn to my blind side.

I always cover my head with my hand which is the side turning into. My elbow pointed down. I can't begin to tell you how many times I have witnessed fists flying over my head when doing this.

Like I said before peoples first natural instinct is to hit what they don't like and of course that is your face. The face represents everything negative or positive a person hates. Attached too the face is the mouth that has a horrible sound that comes out of it. All a person is thinking is how can I shut that thing up.

I also will hold my fingers together and strike towards the eyes. This will disrupt his vision. An opponent who cant see is one who cannot attack you. This movement is also one that you can use to attack from any angle. The main purpose is to gain a split second of time and cause brief pain.

I also would try and throw one of the guys towards their buddies. By doing This it is putting an unconscious or dazed person between myself and an enemy. Doing this has also made it where they hit their own friend too. There is a definite strategy in fighting multiple people.

The most important strikes are ones that affect their breathing, eyesight, or crippling. If they can't breathe, they can't fight. If they can't see, they don't know where to hit so they can't fight. If they can't walk, they can't chase after you. So, they can't fight.

FIGHTING RANGES

FIGHTING RANGES

To be a well-rounded martial artist. I feel a person needs to be proficient in all four ranges of fighting with weapons and empty hand. The first range is kicking. This means someone within a distance of your feet. The second range is boxing. This means a person within the range of hands, and knees. The third range is trapping. This means a person within the range of head butt, elbows, knees, shoulders, biting etc. the fourth range is grappling. This range is on the ground utilizing your whole body as a weapon, leg locks, elbow locks, arm bars, and chokes etc.

KICKING RANGE

BOXING RANGE

TRAPPING RANGE

GRAPPLING RANGE

The Beginning Stages of My Martial Life

I started my grappling range at age 6 in wrestling. Wrestling was a great attribute in developing my base, center, and of course explosiveness. I was honored to learn wrestling from Ernie (Red Dog) Johnson. **Ernie Johnson (191lbs) was Scappoose Oregon's first state wrestling champion in 1956.** Ernie taught me so many great things as a kid. How to workout out and make your core strong. How to use other peoples energy against themselves. Strength training and cardio was his big thing. He would always say the worst way to loose was to loose your cardio and feel helpless. It didn't matter what your skill was if you couldn't move you couldn't react.

Ernie was famous for his cradle and cross face ankle throw. One of the big transition moves was from cradle to a half nelson.

Ernie was my coach in wrestling from 6 years old thru to high school. He brought me to many tournaments. I would wrestle year round in collegiate, free style, and Greco Roman. Greco Roman was my favorite because it was all about throws. I loved to throw people. Ernie taught the head and arm and belly to back. I cant say enough good things about wrestling and what it did for me.

RIP Ernie Red Dog Johnson

My dad never had any formal training in fighting other than he was a great baseball player and a veteran. He had really fast hands and loved to play slap box with me. I've always heard stories of how my dad was not someone to tangle with. His reputation for being a street fighter was definitely earned.

I loved to put the boxing gloves on and go against him. He always took it easy on me but he made me feel like I was kicking but. My dad was a great teacher. He knew how to teach and let you control the level of speed and power.

When I started to get professional training in both wrestling and boxing my dad was very excited and supportive. I loved that us kids could defend ourselves. My dad hated bullies with a passion. He would always say no one has the right to lay hands on you and you always stick up for the under dog. As long as you do that I will always have your back and support you. My dad also said if I ever hear of you starting a fight "Ill kick your ass".

RIP dad love you

Kenneth Wayne Mather

So my boxing range started by age 8. By none other than the #1 contender in the world Richard "sweet" Sue. Boxing helped by developing my footwork and hand speed. It teaches you to move your body with your hands and feet. I feel boxing is the hardest to teach out of all the arts.

RIP Richard "Sweet" Sue

My first lesson in kicking range was karate and taekwondo. This education came from Marty Maye. Those systems are what is considered a hard style. Karate and TKD taught me bone breaking power with both my hands and feet. Unlike boxing, you condition your hands and feet to be able to break bricks, boards, ice, and/or people. By the age of 16 I received my black belt and was already competing quite a bit at tournaments and had a good number of street fights by this age.

Marty Maye and me

At age 13 Marty and I use to go and visit Sifu Al Dacascos's school in Beaverton. I really was attracted to the movements of Sifu Al . We would go to his school for open spar nights on Friday. Sifu Al Dacascos would always pull me aside and show me inside trapping range with multiple combinations of attack. I was instantly in love with the system. So, this is where I started my experience in the trapping range. I had a great base, I was light on my feet, I had fast hands, I had terrific power. But I was still missing fluidity. That's where the trapping range of Wun Hop Kuen Do came in. I continually still always trained in my other systems. This just was another attribute to add to my martial life.

GM Al Dacascos

Eventually I met Guro John Daniels and started my FMA training. I would stay the weekends at his house and train religiously both days on sticks, knives, Muay Thai, and JKD. Really loved the focus on elbows and knees. This helped me in covering all ranges including weapons. That again is only a brief explanation of how I started my martial arts training and all ranges of combat.

Guro John Daniels and myself

Personal Experience

Factual Situations

SITUATION 1

My first experience with Jackals started at the young age of 8 years old. We were in the 4th grade and there were a group of 6th grade bullies that corner the younger kids and beat them up. They would take their money. This also happened to me and my best friend, Travis Sue. Well, we figured out in order to beat these big kids we would have to team up and take them on together. There was about 8 of them all together. Back then, not a lot of supervision outside playground or by the bathrooms. We waited until a bully would go into the bathroom and we would follow in and jump him. After doing that a couple times we realized there was really only one tough guy and he was the wolf. Most of the jackals quit once a couple of their buddies got beat up. The leader was tough. One recess I seen the bully and he was looking for us. He spotted Travis and vee lined for him. He didn't see me. When he approached Travis, I jumped on his back holding him in a choke while Travis started punching him in his face. This was the end of the bullying situation. This was a prime example of a wolf who lost his way leading jackals down the wrong path in life.

SITUATION 2

Another time I experienced 3 wolves, guys that had each other's back and didn't stop unless all was lost. I was driving down highway 30 travel through St. Helens. This was a 4-lane highway. I was in the far-left lane speed limit was 45. There was a car to the right of me and I notice 3 motorcycles coming up fast.

They went around me into oncoming traffic with no regard to vehicles coming towards them. A lady in the oncoming traffic swerved to miss the bikes and almost wrecked her car and cause another to go off the road and back on. I came up to the motorcycles and said a few choice words. They said "pull over," So I did. I pulled into a big parking lot. I jumped out of my truck and two of the bikes came to a stop. The first two jumped off. They started to charge me. One of them had his helmet off. The other guys were still wearing theirs. The guy with the helmet off tried to hit me with his helmet in a back hand motion. I ducked and immediately threw a right cross and hit the second guy with the helmet on, smashing the visor. This knocked him to the ground. As soon as I punched that guy, I turned to face the first guy and threw a right cross smashing him in the face. Before he hit the ground, I grabbed him by the hair pulled towards me and pushed his head while taking his feet out. This allowed to bounce the basketball (head) on the concrete.

The second guy was just getting back up and I rushed over and football kicked him in the neck. The 3rd motorcycle just parked and started to get off and I ran over did a flying sidekick knocking him off his bike onto the ground and his bike fell next to him. I then stomped on his forehead and he said he had enough. Three wolves down. The reason I say three wolves down is because none of them backed down until the end.

SITUATION 3

This is one example of many. The year was 2007 my wife, David Brandon AKA "the big Indian", Brian and I entered a lounge bar in Warrenton, Oregon called South Jetty Bar. This is a big tourist place on the Oregon coast. We had just ordered our drinks and sat down. It was karaoke night. My friend, the big Indian (David Brandon), loved to have fun and sing when he's been drinking. David is a Marine vet and also a very skilled martial artist. Someone was singing David's favorite song. I think it was Eddie Money song. Anyways, he went out on the floor and started to sing with the guy. They were both having a blast.

Well then, the big Indian jumped up and stomped to the beat of music. Well, David is 300 + lbs. The cd skipped. This made the song stop. The guy was fine they gave each other a high five and he came over and sat down. The other guy was with a group of 12 and had a girlfriend who was in a leg cast. You could tell they all been drinking all day. I overheard the girlfriend saying to him "Are you going to let some fucker, fuck your song up?" She kept egging him on until he final came over to our table and said something. David immediately jumped up and said he was sorry and offered to buy him a drink. He said "Cool".

So, we thought it was done and fine. Then he comes back saying "No, you need to buy all of us a drink." I then stepped up and said "Fuck no! Everything was fine until your girlfriend kept on. We all are here to have a good time. David didn't mean to ruin your song." I turned to my wife, David, Brian and asked them to pay our bill. I knew this was only going to escalate because he had a couple guys by the exit. While they were paying the bill, I walked over to the group and confronted the main guy. I positioned myself between two pool tables and the main guy in front of me with all his friends. No one was behind me. I said "Look, we are leaving. Have a good night." Of course, I'm facing him at a 45-degree angle hands up while talking open palms facing him. His response was "You owe us all drinks." Now I'm pissed. I can see it was going to be a problem. I said "We are leaving and you're not getting shit!".

As I'm talking to him, I'm letting my left hand down slightly and showing him my chin. I knew because of his body language that he was right-handed. I knew he would swing for my face. Why? Because that's what he didn't like. Which he did. So, he swung with his right fist. I passed the punch, (like a catcher holding mitt catching a fist and deflecting it away from your face) grabbed him by the ears, head butted him in the bridge of nose like 10 times. Then I smashed his face on edge of pool table. I then changed directions and, of course, covered my head while turning. While in motion as I turned, I could see fists fly over my head, one from opposite directions. The first person I saw while turning, I side kicked his knee breaking it, folding it backwards. Then I immediately turned back to punch another guy in the throat. So now that's three down. I elbowed a 4th person with a right elbow to the jaw he was approaching me from the back. I followed with a left cross to the same jaw. He was out. Now that's four wolves down. This all happened very fast. By this time the bouncers have stepped in to break it up. Three wolves took an ambulance ride.

David

(The Big Indian)

Brandon

RIP

SITUATION 4

This is a 'What if?" factor. It was 1989 my brother was in the Coast Guard. We decided to go visit him for spring break. It was at Seaside, Oregon. Everyone's favorite thing to do was cruise the strip in your cars or walk. We decided to walk. As we were walking across the Safeway parking lot, It was not lit up very well, Somewhat dark. Five guys approached us as we walked by them it seemed ok. Everyone was there to have a good time. Unfortunately, those guys had a different plan. I hear someone running up behind us. I turned to look and "BAMMMM!"- a guy hit me with brass knuckles. I didn't go down. Instead, it made furious with rage.

I went into BERSERKER mode. I lit through that guy like a class five tornado. I grabbed him by the throat running him backwards while continuously punching him in the face. I bet we were 50 yards from where it started because the pressure, I was putting on him. Then I smashed his head right on the concrete. In the meantime, my brother was fighting two guys. Just as the main guy hit the concrete, I get up to turn. Luckily my hands were up because this guy had a stick and swung it at me.

I grabbed the stick and punched the guy like five times in the face. He hit the ground so I football kicked his face, too. I raced towards my brother. He knocked one guy out and was getting ready to fight the other two.

I ran as fast as I could jumping up in the air and did a flying side kick to the back of one of the guys Just as my brother hit the other guy with a hard right cross. My guy was down so I focused on the guy my brother just hit. I grabbed him by the back of the hair yanking him off his feet so I could stomp his face. The fifth guy was a pussy - never really got involved. In this incident there were four wolves and one jackal. The jackals always run.

SITUATION 5

When I was around 19. I experienced my first experience of never sitting with my back to any entrance. I was sitting with a bro in north Portland and having lunch. And two other guys. My back was to the entrance. They were just talking and carrying on, not paying attention to anything around them or us. I was just listening to them talk and chiming in when needed. Out of nowhere a man explodes between myself and another guy stabbing the guy sitting next to my bro. We both grabbed the guy and beat the living shit out of him. It opened my eyes to always be aware of my surroundings. The guy lived. Actual they both did. The bad guy ended up in the hospital for a while.

Situation 6

This is another reason why I always look behind myself before entering any room or closed off area. This was Jan 2022 I went to dinner with my family to a local family restaurant/bar. We were there for about an hour. We ordered our food and had the opportunity to drink one drink. I was just getting up to use the restroom which was about 20 feet from our table. As I'm walking towards the door, I look back, like always, because I trust no one. I see this big guy charging towards me at the bathroom coming down from the bar. I of course get into my READY POSITION and yell at the guy "WOOOOW! WOOOW! SLOW YOUR ROLL WHATS UP? ". He had this hatred anger on his face like he wanted to kill me. He stops and again I say "WHATS YOUR PROBLEM?" He then swings at me and I could tell from his body language and how he held himself that it was coming from his right side. I straight lined him with a left lead to the throat. Grabbing his throat and squeezing as I'm pushing him back on his heels. A person can't throw punches or kicks while back stepping on their heels. Then I threw a right cross hitting him in the eye socket knocking his ass out on the ground. The shocking thing for my kids and their fiancés was the realism of why and did that really just happen. Like I told them, always be ready. You never know when a wolf whose lost his path will strike. That is the most dangerous kind of wolf.

AWARENESS

So, let me first start with awareness. Being aware of your surroundings and how to read people. Also understanding body positioning. Regardless of any situation understanding how to position yourself for any situation is 90 % of the battle.

Learn how to read people. Watch what hand they drink with. What hand they smoke with. If they are on the phone, what hand holds the phone and what hand is writing? When they take a step in any direction what foot do they lead with? What hand do they use to open the door, etc? these are all ways to learn what hand is the dominate hand. Reading people is a must A great example would be what hand a person holds his/her phone in while talking on it. Most people keep their dominate hand free so they can do activities while talking. Like taking notes on a piece of paper, opening a door etc. Being aware of your own actions and habits will help you better understand other peoples movements

I will tell you how I position myself in everyday life so you can get a better understanding of how I think 24/7. When I walk out the door of my house or go into any building, where I sit, what I do before going into any enclosed room or space. I look around myself and in the back seat before I get into my vehicle.

I always sit where I can view any exit or entrance, especially entrance. This way I can observe any person coming in. If I'm with someone, especially my wife, I always position them or her so I can have their back. I also try to choose a seat that no one can sit behind me.

you never know when or where the element of surprise can happen. A person might think it sounds like paranoia. I can truly tell you it is not the case. I would just rather be prepared for a situation that is unexpected than not be prepared and wish I were. Like the old saying "Better to be a warrior in a garden than a gardener in a war". When I walk down the street with my wife or anyone for that matter, I always put myself between them and any other person coming from the other direction. This way I'm in control of the range and can read any threat. When being approached by a person weather he might be hostile or not.

Keeping a person out of harms way

My body position is a 45-degree angle and hands up palms facing them like I'm going to catch a basketball as to say stop without saying stop and a smile on my face. From a cameras perspective I want to appear harmless or non-threatening. I am always standing on the balls of my feet with my knees slightly bent so If my bubble is breached my hands are ready to pass, parry, or strike with split second response.

Ready stance

Since I'm on my balls of my feet than calves are flexed ready to spring in any direction. I call that the springs of life.

My study has brought me to the conclusion that 95% of a people first strike is the thing they hate the most. That is your face. The ugly voice hole.

Most the people you'll run across that are willing to perform this threat are usually untrained. What I mean by untrained is a professional martial arts school. This doesn't mean they don't know how to fight. I've met and have plenty of friends that are tough street fighters and would beat the shit out of most highly trained martial artist. It means they were never taught the full attributes of what the code is to make a great warrior. In today's day, the criminals and villains are training just as much as people going to martial arts school, because you can find anything on the YouTube or social media.

Hitting what we don't like THE FACE

Another important thing is to always evaluate your perimeter. There might be an object you can slam your enemy into. This object can also be used as an obstacle once the fight starts for your enemy will have to maneuver around to get to you. This could allow you a second or two to reestablish your defense or attack.

Smashing face on a table edge

Another thing is the ground you're standing on, is it sand, concrete, dirt, gravel, ice, or grass? If it's sand, the perfect thing to blind your enemy by throwing sand in their eyes or if you end up on the ground put it in their face.

If it is concrete, that's a hard service to make them land on. It's also like 20 grit sand paper. Rake their face across it after you smash their head.

Playing in the sand

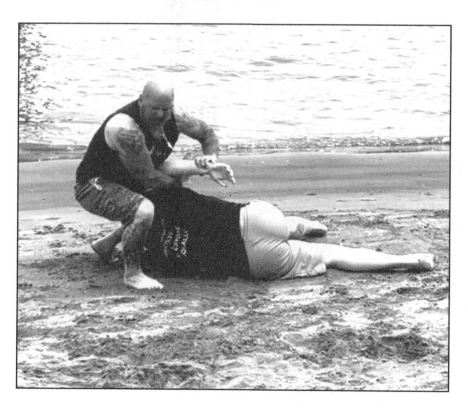

If it's dirt it has the same attributes as sands great for blinding or choking your opponent.

If it's gravels, depending on the size of gravel, smashing someone's face in it will get it in their eyes and mouth. It can be used as a long rage weapon. Small rocks thrown hard enough can hurt or knock out a person. Also, it can be a great distraction. ABCs-attack by combination.

If it's ice. Ice is very hard and extremely slippery so your moves should be evenly balanced, types of moves using this to your advantage.

Playing the snow.

If it is grass. It could be slippery, muddy and hard so it has more attributes you can use to your advantage.

You can't always pick your perfect platform so that is why I choose to train my students outside any chance I can, in the grass, on the concrete, in the water. So many schools forget the meaning of what *Martial* means. It basically means military, army, and war. So why would you train on a padded floor in a GI. That is not reality. When is the last time you had a person threaten you with a GI on or on a padded floor? It's usually t-shirt, shorts, jeans, boots etc.

The GRINCH taking on another in a GI

Statistically, under tense situation your brain remembers only a few instinctive moves by habit. So, if you train for a person who only wears a GI or heavy belt on, then how will you instinctively know how to deal with a person in shorts and a t-shirt? There isn't a sleeve to grab or a belt. So, you are preparing yourself for unrealistic situations. Then if they do have a jacket on or a hoodie, this is just a bonus. Also, most assailants will be wearing shoes or boots. This means even the unskilled person now has weapons on their feet. So again, train as though your opponent has boots on. This way, you're always expecting the unexpected. The key is train for reality of what people wear. What if a weapon is pulled? I personally always carry a blade or two or three. 3 blades are what I usually carry. One for my brother, one to throw away, and one to use.

Knife being thrown towards the eyes

Knife entry—slicing the throat—Parry and slice weapon hand– carry weapon hand over in the trough– then disarm by cutting blade out

After disarm, then stab the body.

Finally cut your way out as you step back

Remember this, anything could be a weapon. Maybe you only have your car keys. The keys fit nicely between your fingers. Great for striking at the eyes. Remember, if they can't see they can't fight. I personally always have a weapon on my key ring too. I have a deer horn on a quick release on one set of keys. I have a blade on another set.

Holding a set of keys for striking

Your surroundings are key. You might see a bottle, a rock, a chair etc. Use your environment. Using a projectile object can also be used as an ABC attack, Attack By Combination. Throwing an object at one guy while striking another or throwing at same person followed by a strike is a great entry.

Throwing sand in the face
then follow with a punch

What if you are approached by multiple people while with your wife? How do you protect your wife while defending yourself at the same time? This is also talked about and trained. Always put yourself between the threat and your wife or significant other. Also, educate them on when the fight starts they need to get somewhere safe, especially if they are not trained on how to fight. My wife, of course is trained and has been in a few situations like that with me.

I look at every situation as to how would I react if someone approached my friend/kids/brother/wife. How fast would I "snatch the breath out of someone?" What I mean is if I was with a friend and someone approached him in a negative manner how fast would I react to aid him, whether it means controlling the approaching person or knocking him the fuck out. That's what I think about when I'm being approached by multiple people.

I assume that everyone has the same process and they live by the code I do. So, in a sense, I'm fighting myself. The question has been asked, How many street fights have I been in? The most honest answer is too many to count. I would say that 95 % of all the fights I've been in were against 2 or more assailants. I can't think of any of them being similar to each other.

There really isn't a perfect answer or road map to success. The only thing you can do is prepare for the unexpected. Try to add statistics in the equation of your training. Fighting one person vs multiple attackers is like comparing night to day. When dealing with one person. That person is In front is your only focus

Dealing with multiple people, the "what if?" factor is in play. The unexpected, the unforeseen, the blind spot. The multiples of fist or weapons coming at you from all angles.

Dealing with multiple attackers

So, yes, fighting one person to me is like a regular sparring class. A walk in the park. Fighting multiple people is like playing Russian roulette. The odds are against you from the start. The most dangerous part about fighting multiple people is what you can't see. Because if he can touch you, he can kill you.

I feel personally there are very few instructors that are qualified to teach students how to defend against one assailant. An even smaller percentage are qualified to teach a student against multiple attackers or assailants. Most instructors have never been in the position of defending themselves in a life-or-death situation. Everything you've been taught must become second nature, habit, instinctive, a split-second action that causes the most pain with little exposure while always ready for what's next.

MY TIME WITH THE HELLS ANGELS and SECURITY

Some of my experience dealing with wolves on a professional level is doing security work for the Hells Angels. The reason I say wolves is because they are a group of guys who not only have each other's back but will never back down or quit unless they are all dead...period. Doing security for this type of group attracts other groups of like nature so you have to understand how they think, act, and move. I won't give any events or times. Just understand I wouldn't have been put in that situation if I didn't earn their respect and trust to make sure things were handled accordingly without prejudice and very efficient.

HELLS ANGELS AND ME

HELLS ANGELS AND ME

Hells Angels and me

Hells Angels and me

HELLS ANGELS AND ME

SECURITY

HAPPY from SONS He was also a Hells Angel

SECURITY

HELLS ANGELS AND ME

HELLS ANGELS AND ME

HELLS ANGELS AND ME

Awareness and What I Carry

I've been asked why do I carry any weapons at all considering the skill set I have. My answer to carrying weapons is I would rather have them and not need them than need them and not have them. A weapon is only as good as the person who is wielding it, so training every day is a must.

Reaction time is everything. Being proficient and precise is a must because you only have that split second to gain the upper hand before the second, third, fourth etc. person makes his move to end you . I designed a special type of knife and sheath that I carry everyday. The knife is a fixed blade that wields itself well for both slicing, stabbing, and parrying. It can be held very comfortably in both fencing (cooking) position blade forward and icepick (killing) position blade backward. The sheath that holds my blade has a special purpose. I call the sheath "the Soul Keeper" . It is design so the handle is facing downward so it can be drawn like a gun slinger, very fast and proficient in a killing position ready for battle.

Picture of my blade

Understand the wolf and the jackal both attack with the intent to inflict extreme pain. It is not like the movies; they don't attack one at a time, EVER! They attack all at once and as fast as they can. Put yourself in this perspective if you were with your friend and someone or a group approaches him/her with a negative demeanor. How fast would you move to aide or have your friends back now multiply that 10x because these guys do this all the time. This is how you train to deal with multiple attackers.

I've been asked many times about going to the ground in a street fight. I spent most of my life wrestling. I did this for the sport, knowledge, and physical fitness. Wrestling is the most exhausting sport out there. Wrestling utilizes every muscle in your body with full exertion. I also received my blue belt in BJJ so I have the knowledge to defend against BJJ practitioners. The advantage of learning to wrestle it teaches you balance and great foot work. Because I know the difference between sport and street. I never go to the ground in a street fight unless it is accidental. I avoid the ground at all costs. If I hit the ground, my goal is to make sure they hit first. I trained very religiously in grappling. So, I can avoid going to the ground and defending against a grappling technique. If you take the fight to the ground, I can 100% guarantee that the friend of assailant will curb stomp your head. Staying on your feet is the only option for surviving on the street.

PICTURE OF ME CURB STOMPING SOMEONES HEAD. THIS IS GUARANTEED TO HAPPEN IF YOU GO TO THE GROUND FIGHTING MULTIPLE PEOPLE. WHILE YOUR ON THE GROUND HIS BUDDY WILL FOOTBALL KICK OR STOMP YOUR HEAD

How do you train to deal with real life conflict? You must make your first moves/strikes damaging. You don't have time to play with one person. If you spend too much time with one person his friend will truly smash you. So, I recommend doing speed drills in your school, reaction drills with your most damaging attack. But never just stop. Always follow with a quarter turn or half turn with covering your head while keeping your original target in sight. Train with obstacles in your path and learn how to use them for your advantage. Train outside in an environment that is realistic with realistic clothes on.

Utilizing the obstacle that was between us

How does a person train to stay off the ground? I feel a person needs to be proficient in wrestling or BJJ. But That is not enough. A person also has to be proficient in boxing, kickboxing, karate/Tae Kwon Do, kung fu, Filipino martial arts or for me a well-rounded martial art Kajukenbo/Wun Hop Kuen Do. Also train as though your opponent has knives on his hands and feet so understanding range is very important being very quick and evasive. Learning to stick and move being light on your toes using what I call *the springs of life.*

Pictures of fighting stance with heel slightly lifted

SPRINGS OF LIFE

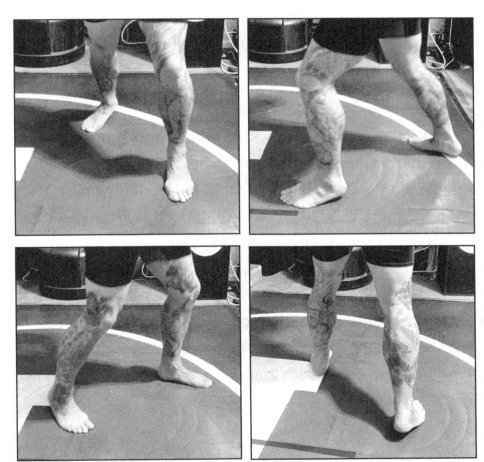

The three ways to train are sight, sound, and feel

Training with sight is a very popular way with most gyms and facilities. An example of this would be hitting the mitts or heavy bag. When your training partner holds a mitt, you fire working on your reaction time. Another example of this is sparring. Watching your opponent's movement and working on your timing of when to attack or counter.

Training with sound is also a very popular way. An example of this is the bell or whistle. Your trainer blows the whistle, then you react. You hear the bell go off, you react. Your trainers voice, you react.

Training with feel is a whole different style or aspect. I think it helps cater more towards street fighting personally. An example of this is putting a blind fold on and hitting mitts. Your jab is more used to feel where the mitt is located. Rather then striking with the jab with power your using it to trap. Once you feel where the mitt is, you trap the mitt while striking the mitt with your other hand. What I use to tell my students is you can always strike your own hand. If one of your hands are holding a part of the body you cant miss it, just hit your own hand. Same with grappling you feel your opponent . Hit what you feel.

Making your body quick with split second response time is so very important. One way to do this is the way my Sifu (Al Dacascos) showed me. Its called movie frame fighting. How its done is every time the frame changes to a new character you react right when you see it. doesn't matter what move your working on. When you see the frame change EXPLODE like a canon.

Movie frame fighting

Maybe you set up two of your punching dummies. I like to use BOBS. Turn a movie on. It could be a love movie. No sound just watch and react. Work on your multi person attacks . When the frame changes work on attacks that would take out two or more people only stop when you know you have successfully achieved a goal . Zero hesitation zero pause and continuous flow. I will also keep one of my BOBS half empty in the base so I can easily throw it around. Striking it and throwing it into another BOB. Practice using their own guys against themselves. You can set up three dummies and do the same thing. Continuously striking and moving while throwing strikes and grabbing dummies

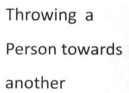

Throwing a Person towards another

Remember how you train is how you will perform in real life. There is no do over . A mistake can mean your life . Another way to train can be a ringer or bell . So this way your now relying on sound verses site. Setting the bell to go off every 20 sec . The anticipation to explode.

Again right after the technic is delivered always be ready for an attack than reset to do it again. Don't be afraid to put obstacles in your way such as a chair, table, etc. Also try all these drills outside in the grass, on the sand, on gravel, and in the water. Again real life training is the best training .

Always using your surroundings . Outside could have trees in your way or a big rock . If its in your way its also in their way. Thinking about how to use those objects to your advantage. This will give you the upper hand. I don't look at objects as a hindrance. I look at it as my advantage over my enemy.

A warrior trains for all situations. Let no circumstance be the influence of your fear. **LET YOUR FEAR BE THE INFLUENCE IN YOUR TRAINING.**

FMA (Filipino martial arts) training

When training your trapping range and incorporating weapons. Think about the actual weapon coming at you. It could be a base ball bat, a beer bottle, a tire iron , a cue stick etc. anything can be a weapon so practice with everything. go through drills holding a beer bottle or a tire iron. The element of surprise should be with the assailant not with you.

What if a guy comes at you wielding a blade? You don't have a way to get by him or get away. One thing you could do is slip your shoes off and use them as mitts to smack the blade away while simultaneously smashing him in the face. You could grab a chair if your in a bar or restaurant. Using the legs of the chair as a means to stab at him or cause damage while you attack him.

Using the chair as an ABC (attack by combination)

In a bar or restaurant is also a place where you can use a projectile attack. The salt and pepper container could be thrown at the person while simultaneously attacking with an explosive blow. They might have Tabasco sauce something when your in close if its on your hands rub it in his face while attacking him. Hot sauce in the eyes can be brutal to be able to see.

Hot sauce bottle/beer bottle across the head

If your outside and there are rocks on the ground. Rocks works great for entry attacks. Your on the beach, kick sand towards your assailant as your following in for the attack. Again there are always options to gain the upper hand but you must look for it and train for it. Its about survival and going home at night. If a person is willing to assault you. There is no way to judge what level of harm he or they are willing to do to you.

You are your first responder. You are your first line of defense for yourself and your family. Your only a victim if you choose to be one.

Throwing sand in the face of attacker

Wounded Wolf

The wounded wolf is probably the most dangerous. It covers the two areas of pain. These areas are physical, and psychological . The psychological could include sad, happy, and fear. The physical aspect would be injury to ones self.

An example of a psychological situation would be loss of a loved one and reacting from the pain. Maybe a retaliation against the cause or reaction to someone rubbing you the wrong way. It could also be someone attacking a loved one so the reaction is out of control driven by both love and fear. What makes this kind of wolf so dangerous is reacting with zero worry about consequence. To win at all costs. Some wolves are raised with the most important aspect of the code "heart".

An example of physical would be a person who has maybe a broken arm, leg, etc. Having some kind of disability. This doesn't make him weak. He is aware of his disability. This just makes his other areas stronger. Being backed into a corner the wolf has no choice but to survive at all cost.

Never under estimate your opponent because appearance can be deceiving

TECHNIQUES

READY POSITION
1. Standing at a 45-degree angle facing your assailant.
2. Hands up with palms outward as if to catch a basketball.
3. Elbows down this also helps protect your side.
4. Whatever lead foot you favor that is forward so is that lead hand.
5. Pretend there is a nail on the top of your head and the top of the assailants with a string attached from yours to his.
6. Always position yourself so that your hands or your feet are never in a straight plane or on same side of string.
7. This position is the most non-confrontational state to be in but also the deadliest. You are in a position to catch, parry. Pass, and/or strike

READY POSITION

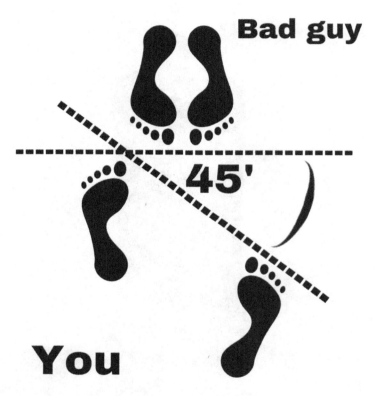

READY STANCE FOOTWORK

SITUATIONAL TUTORIAL

Keeping a loved one safe and using your environment

Me seeing the assailant and pointing to stay between the car and action

The assailant has a knife he's hiding on his right side. My knife is on my right always ready for a quick draw for defense

Continuing with technique as he slices at me I parry his blade hand while simultaneously hitting him in the throat

Then smash his head against car

Knee to his face then I strip his blade

After stripping the blade I follow with a inward slice

Finally a knee to the face

Attack by ABC's
Throwing sand at the eyes blinding the assailant

Attacking the throat / destroying his breathing

 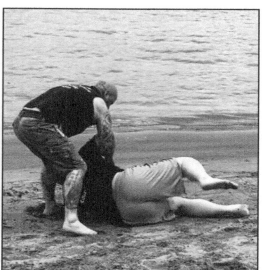

Attacking the eyes again at the same time pulling him backwards . Slamming his head on the ground followed by my knee to the face. Putting his arm in a Kimura and snapping his shoulder ready and awaiting any of his friends

Assailant with a weapon

Attack the eyes with sand

Followed by controlling the weapon

Attacking the throat so they cant breath

Breaking the knee so he can't walk

Stripping the weapon

Using his own weapon against him

The finishing blows

Finishing blow while maintaining control of his hand

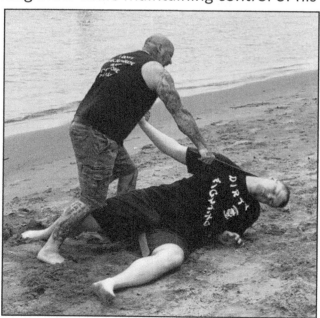

ABC's attack

Sand to the face

Trapping the hands followed by head butt bridge of nose

After head butt to bridge of nose maintain control

Attacking the throat while still maintaining control

While maintaining control curb stomp the face

REST IN PEACE

ATTACK BY COMBINATION

Using a bottle as first entry

First attacker out of the way, hit the next attacker in the throat disabling his breath

USING OBJECTS AROUND YOU

After I disable his breath, I grab him by the back of his head and slam his face against the table.

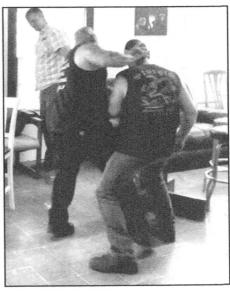

After the head smash I turn and attack the other attacker

Followed by a quick blow to the knee

Another combo attack

Hit the throat

Left palm slap to ear while grabbing the neck for a head butt

Hit him in the throat while tripping him, turning to face other attacker as he punches I parry the hand

Left throat punch while holding his right hand

Attack the knee than push him away to go after third person

As he throws a punch I Pass and attack the arm

Turning so I can see the other attackers

I take out his wind

When he hits the ground I apply a Kimura, breaking his shoulder keeping my eye on my surroundings

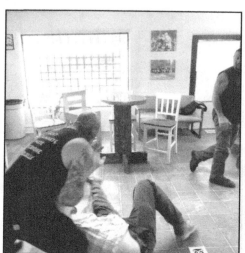
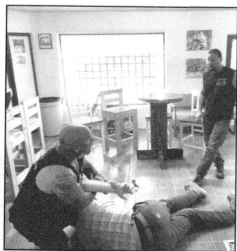

After breaking the shoulder I stomp the head on my way to meet the first attacker

I attack the eyes , left hook to the chin, knee to the ribs while holding his arm

Left palm to the ear while grabbing his head

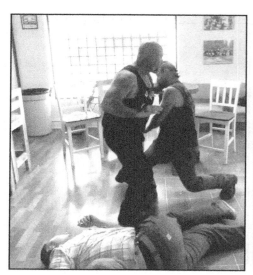

A final head butt to put his ass to sleep

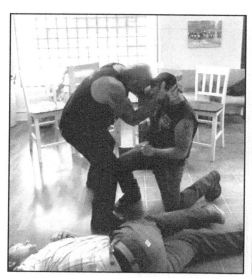

Using Your Surroundings

Approached by three guys with knives

I hit the closest guy with a chair

Pull my blade and parry his knife hand with it

As I parry I hit the attacker in the throat and than slice across his throat with my blade

Cutting and disarming his blade by slicing it out

The third attacks with his left. I parry the blade punch him in the throat and then slice his throat

Disarm by slicing the weapon out of his hand

Adjusting necks and breaking knees

Its called getting off the motorcycle, hooking the chin, pulling back while spinning with a side kick

Breaking the knee followed by throat punch

Finish him off with an elbow strike to the jaw followed by knee to the face

1. DUCK AND COVER
2. What direction I am turning towards or going into danger. That lead hand palm covers ear, chin down, and elbow pointed down.
3. When turning, pivot on balls of feet, towards the side of cover.
4. Keep your back straight, bend at the knees using all legs (DO NOT BEND OVER AT HIPS)
5. Whenever turning to face any direction always cover
6. Always ready to explode at every point using your legs for momentum.

FOR DEMENSTRATION PICTURES ON NEXT PAGE

Training in different Environments

1. Trap to disarm

Training in a foot of snow and it's 15 degree out. Real life training. Nothing beats it

2. Go for supporting leg

3. Take down

4. Disable with own weapon

TRAINING ON THE GRASS

Notice my knee is on his head and I'm ready to snap his shoulder to take on next person

TRAINING ON THE BEACH
W/ Guro John Daniels

WOLVES

BIKERS (wolves)

BIKERS (wolves)

WOLVES

I am my brother's keeper

MY TEAMMATES

MY BROTHERS

WOLVES

Left to right

Tim Gustavson, myself, Marty Maye, and Mike Rethati

Out of all the instructors, coaches, and mentors in my life. Nothing compared to the skills and attributes we developed while training with each other. Over 25 years of sparring and influencing one another.

WOLVES

Myself and Ronin

I am my brother's keeper

Warriors to the core

WOLVES

Left to right front

Myself, Rod Coulter, Kelly Worden, Prof Trigg

Left to right back

Martin Gonzalez, Jeff, Tim Gustavson,

Bob Anderson, Belton Lubas

BIKERS

Training and having fun (wolves)

Training with Guro Dan Inosanto and Guro John Daniels. This is something that would happen three times a year. A martial art school would host Guro Dan if it was close enough we would definitely make it. Guro Dan Inosanto was one of Bruce Lees top students. I feel very blessed to have trained with him many times over the years. John Daniels has played a huge part in my martial knowledge

SIFU AL DACASCOS AND ME

Marty Maye is my first true martial arts instructor. I met him when I was 12-13 years old. We fought in tournaments together all over the US and Canada. We've been beating on each other ever since. I learned more from him overall than anyone To this day. We are forever brothers.

RICHARD (SWEET) SUE

#1 contender in the world for many years

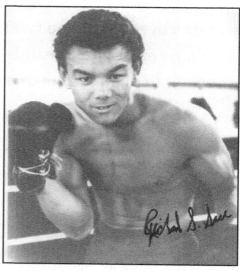

Richard and Travis teaching boxing at my outdoor martial arts camp

Travis Sue has been my close brother since the fourth grade . We wrestled together. We boxed together. We cried together. This a very special picture to me. We are standing in front of my dads honor wall holding both of our dads celebration of life pamphlet. Travis lives by the same code as I do. I am my brother's keeper. We will always be best of brothers.

JT (the General) Taylor

BJJ Fourth Degree Black Belt

I received my Blue Belt in 2010 from JT, I am now studying under Professor Don Stoner and currently working towards my Purple Belt

My Martial Arts Bio

MY BIO

Sifu Mike Mather is an Extreme Martial Arts Stylist. His training started at the young age of 6 years old in the wrestling arts. Training under Ernie Red Dog Johnson. At age 8 he took on the sport of Boxing and received his coaching under the direct hands of the #1 contender in the world Richard (Sweet) Sue. Ready to advance his style at the age of 11, he began his study of Kung Fu and at 13 he diversified his talent and reach and started training in the style Tae Kwon Do under Master Marty Maye. Sifu Mike received his first Black Belt by the age of 16 in Tae Kwon Do under Grand master Wade Lewis. His dedication and love for the fighting arts has led Sifu Mike to train in a variety of Martial arts since then.

He is currently ranked 5th degree Master in Kyushu jujitsu karate under pressure point expert Grandmaster George Dillman. He is also a 5th degree Master in Tae Kwon Do and a Master in Shaolin Kung Fu under Grandmaster Eric Lee. Holds a 3rd degree Black Belt under Guro John Daniels, who is a full instructor under the great Danny Inosanto in the Filipino combative martial arts which includes Jeet Kune Do, Kali Southern Filipino bladed art, Arnis (Northern Filipino stick art), Eskrido stick and knife art. Sifu Mike also holds a 6th degree Black Belt in Wun Hop Kuen Do under the creator Grand Master Al Dacascos. He holds a 3rd degree Black Belt under Sr. Grandmaster Cacoy Canete in the Doce Pares system. He has earned a blue belt in bjj under the General JT Taylor. Sifu Mike is a world champion full contact fighter holding over 30 national grand titles.

Sifu Mike is still training in his Martial life trying to increase his skill set in jiu jitsu. Primarily under Professor Don Stoner under the great Rigan Machado.

Sifu Mike has dedicated and devoted his entire life to the Arts of fighting. With over 45 years of experience in the Martial Arts he has developed a unique blend of combative Martial Arts that delivers real striking power and force under extreme conditions.

Sifu Mike has worked and trained with the best of the best and most famous Martial Artists in the world. His talents and expertise have led him to work with the Military and various other groups on controlled force and defensive tactics against weapons. Sifu Mike is the sole founder and creator of Mather Martial Arts Academy where he laid his roots down in 1993. He currently teaches Traditional Martial Arts, Mixed Martial Arts, and Wrestling and holds seminars on defensive tactics all over. His constant statement remains the same, "I owe all my training, dedication, devotion, loyalty, honor, integrity, and most important heart to the most inspirational person in my life, my dad.
Without my dad's superior job as a role model and a father none of this would be. This is my love, my passion, and my life. Always has been and always will be."

Thank you, God, for the gifts you've given me.

When on my bike its like I'm back in time a 1000 years in control of a wild horse. It is a piece of me and I am a part of it. Always ready at any moment to do battle. When you ride a motorcycle your exposed to all the elements and debris on the road. I tackle riding like I do martial arts. I am constantly 150% offense as well as a 100% defense. If I need to move for my safety I don't wait for the other vehicle. I just react without hesitation and 100% commitment.

Doing a burnout in front of Warrenton city hall

This is a picture of me holding two blades I made. The one a war hatchet made from albino elk horn for a handle. This way both ends of the weapon are deadly. The other blade is an albino elk eye horn for a handle that also goes to a point. This again allows both ends to be very deadly. When I train I think about being a berserker Viking warrior ready to battle at all cost. In my heart I was born a thousand years to late

My brother Jody Mather
His Opinion of My Martial life

Mikey and I would do rounds of boxing and never get to serious, then I would box Dad and it was kind of the same. Half speed and half power just fun. It was Mikey's turn to have a go with Dad and I remember seeing my Dad's demeanor and intensity change. All of a sudden they were going full speed with real power! I realized at that moment that we were different. They had the coordination and fast twitch muscles and they knew what the other was going to do before they did it. I don't think I ever put the gloves on again.

Our family loved fishing, especially Dad and I. Mikey would go and of course he enjoyed it too but not like we did. His love for fighting drove him in a different direction, instead of fishing and hunting every waking moment he would train in some sort of martial arts. He was a quick study and did very well. That's all he would think about. Mikey had a way about him, he could read people very well, especially when it came to someone bad. I had the privilege to actually stick up for him on a couple of occasions when he was younger. As we got older in life Mikey did the same for me. On more than one occasion we took on multiple people together. There is no one better to count on in battle. Our dad raised us with a code we live with to this day. No one gets left behind and if someone gets hit, it will be me before anyone I'm with.

Jody Mather and Me

Jody with a big buck

WARRIORS CODE

A WARRIOR IS MADE UP OF THESE VIRTUES INTEGRITY, WISDOM, LOYALTY, HONESTY, SKILL, AND HEART.

I MUST HAVE _INTEGRITY_ SO I CAN LIVE BY A CODE WITHIN THYSELF.

I MUST HAVE _WISDOM_ TO HELP MAKE THE RIGHT DECISIONS FOR THE CODE IN LIFE.

I DO NOT STRAY AND I AM ALWAYS _LOYAL_ TO THE CODE.

I NEED TO BE PHYSICALLY FIT AND HAVE THE _SKILL_ TO ALWAYS PROTECT THE CODE

I MUST HAVE _HONESTY_ AND STAND WITH PRIDE FOR THE CODE. I LIVE AND CONDUCT MYSELF WITH GOOD MORALS AND ETHICAL VIRTUES.

A WARRIOR NEVER GIVES UP. WHEN THINGS ARE TOUGH, I NEED _HEART_ TO STAY IN THE FIGHT TILL RIGHT IS RIGHT FOR THE CODE.

MOST IMPORTANT PUT GOD FIRST BECAUSE WITHOUT HIM NOTHING IS POSSIBLE.

Wrote this code in 1993

BERSERKER RUNE

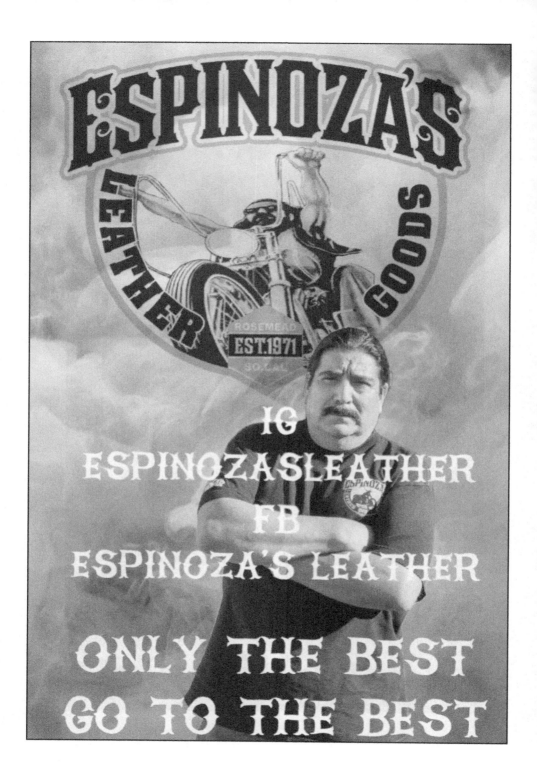

Dacascos Legacy
Through the Eyes of the Warrior

Amazon.com

Grandmaster Al Dacascos

Prof. Dan Andersen

Super Dan Online Library - www.superdanonlinelibrary.com

Over 100 books and videos on site.

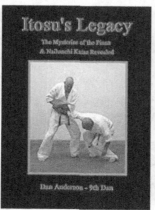

Made in the USA
Middletown, DE
19 May 2024